The babysitter is coming to look after me.

Will she be fat or thin? Will she be tall or small?
I wonder.

Will she like sausages for tea? Or fishfingers and jelly? Or ice cream and chocolate biscuits, and chips?

The babysitter arrives. She has long yellow hair and bright blue boots.

'Say hello to Amy,' says Mummy.
I feel shy, but Amy smiles and looks kind.

'We really must go now,' says Daddy. 'Be good.'

Amy and I wave goodbye.

'What's your cat's name?' asks Amy.
It's Ginger.

'Your hair is gingery, too.' says Amy.

I show Amy my teddy. Teddy and I are hungry.
Amy says, 'It's time for tea.'

'Teddy likes fishfingers. Do you, Amy?'
'Not much,' Amy says.

But Ginger loves fishfingers. He dreams of them in his sleep.

'Come and help me make tea,' says Amy. 'We can
have fishfingers if you like.'

I help find the tea things.
'There's a surprise in the fridge,' says Amy.

It's a wibble-wobble jelly rabbit and ice cream!
I sit up at the table for my tea.

After tea I play with Ginger.

But Ginger is soon tired and starts yawning.
I yawn too.
'Come on, copycat,' says Amy. 'It's bedtime.'

Amy helps me get ready for bed.

She tucks me up. 'I'll be downstairs if you want anything,' she says.

'Good night. Sleep tight. When you wake up,
Mummy and Daddy will be back.'
I say goodnight to Amy. I hope she comes to look
after me again soon.